New York's Government

Kate Schimel and Magdalena Alagna

Rosen Classroom
New York

Published in 2012 by The Rosen Publishing Group, Inc.
29 East 21st Street, New York, NY 10010

Book Design: Chris Brand

Photo Credits: Cover, p. 17 © Shutterstock.com; p. 5 © SuperStock; p. 7 by Jessica Livingston; p. 7 (inset) © Curt Teich Postcard Archives/Archives Photos/Getty Images; p. 9 © The New-York Historical Society; p. 10 (inset) © Hulton/Archive; p. 11 © New York State Archives; p. 13 (inset) © Corbis; p. 13 © Jon Hicks/Corbis; p. 15 © Lee Snider; Lee Snider/Corbis; p. 17 (inset) © New York State Office of General Services; p. 19 © TimePix; p. 21 © Lake County Museum/Corbis.

Library of Congress Cataloging-in-Publication Data

Schimel, Kate.
New York's government / by Kate Schimel and Magdalena Alagna.—1st ed.
p. cm.—(Spotlight on New York)
Includes index.
ISBN: 978-1-4488-5745-6 (lib. bdg.)
ISBN: 978-1-4488-5763-0 (pbk.)
6-pack ISBN: 978-1-4488-5764-7
1. New York (State)—Politics and government—Juvenile literature. I. Alagna, Magdalena. II. Title. III. Series.
JK3416.S24 2012
320.4747—dc22

2011004772

Manufactured in the United States of America

Cover image: This photo shows the Capitol Building in Albany. This striking building was completed in 1899.

Contents

The History of Government in New York State

Government in New York State has grown and changed over the centuries. The first government was created by the Iroquois. They set up a **constitution** hundreds of years ago. In 1626, Dutch **colonists** settled on Manhattan Island. They were still **ruled** by **leaders** who lived in the Netherlands. The British took control in 1664. Then the colonists had to follow English laws. The colonists did not have much say in how their **local government** was run.

In 1776, **representatives** from the **colonies** signed the **Declaration of Independence**. It stated that the colonists no longer wanted to be under British rule. Colonial leaders created a **democracy**, which is a government run by the people. This meant that the colonists could **elect** their own leaders and **vote** on their own **laws**.

The Declaration of Independence was approved in Philadelphia, Pennsylvania, on July 4, 1776. New York's leaders approved it five days later. In this painting, Thomas Jefferson, Benjamin Franklin, and others are shown signing the Declaration of Independence on August 2, 1776. The painting can be seen in the U.S. Capitol Building in Washington, D.C.

Iroquois Government

The Iroquois lived in the area that is now New York State. More than 500 years ago, the Iroquois set up one of the earliest forms of government. Five Iroquois groups, or nations, joined to form the Iroquois League. Iroquois **legend** describes how it happened.

A man named Peacemaker created a constitution for the League with the help of a man named Hayenwatha *(hy-uh-WAH-thuh)* and a woman named Jingosaseh *(gee-GON-sah-say)*. The constitution said that each **nation** could make laws for its own people. However, the League made decisions about matters that concerned everyone, like war.

The League was ruled by a council. The council was made up of leaders from each nation. Council members were chosen by the women who headed the Iroquois **clans**.

The Iroquois League was an early form of democracy. At least once a year, chiefs from each nation of the Iroquois League met to discuss issues that would affect all Iroquois people. The Iroquois constitution was created hundreds of years before the U.S. Constitution was written. Colonial leaders used the laws and rules of the Iroquois League as a model for American democracy. The smaller image shows one artist's idea of what Hayenwatha looked like.

Colonial Government

In 1609, Dutch **merchants** hired an Englishman named Henry Hudson. They wanted him to find a **route** by ship to China. Hudson never found one. He couldn't get around the land surrounding the North Pole. He sailed south and then west and arrived at what is now New York Harbor. Hoping it would lead to the Pacific, Hudson sailed up what we now call the Hudson River and explored the area around it. Hudson claimed that land for the Dutch. The area became known as New Netherland. One of the first Dutch colonies was founded near present-day Albany. Another colony was settled at the tip of Manhattan Island. For many years, New Netherland was ruled by leaders chosen by the Dutch government.

The British took over New Netherland in 1664. King Charles II renamed it New York to honor his brother James, the duke of York. The British ruled New York until the colonies declared their **independence** in 1776. At that time, leaders of the newly formed nation set up a new government.

Albany is about 150 miles up the Hudson River from Manhattan Island. This map, originally created around 1650, shows the locations of both places. At the time, Albany was still a small colony called Fort Orange. New York City was called "Nieuw Amsterdam." A drawing of New York City as it looked in the 1600s can be seen at the bottom of the map.

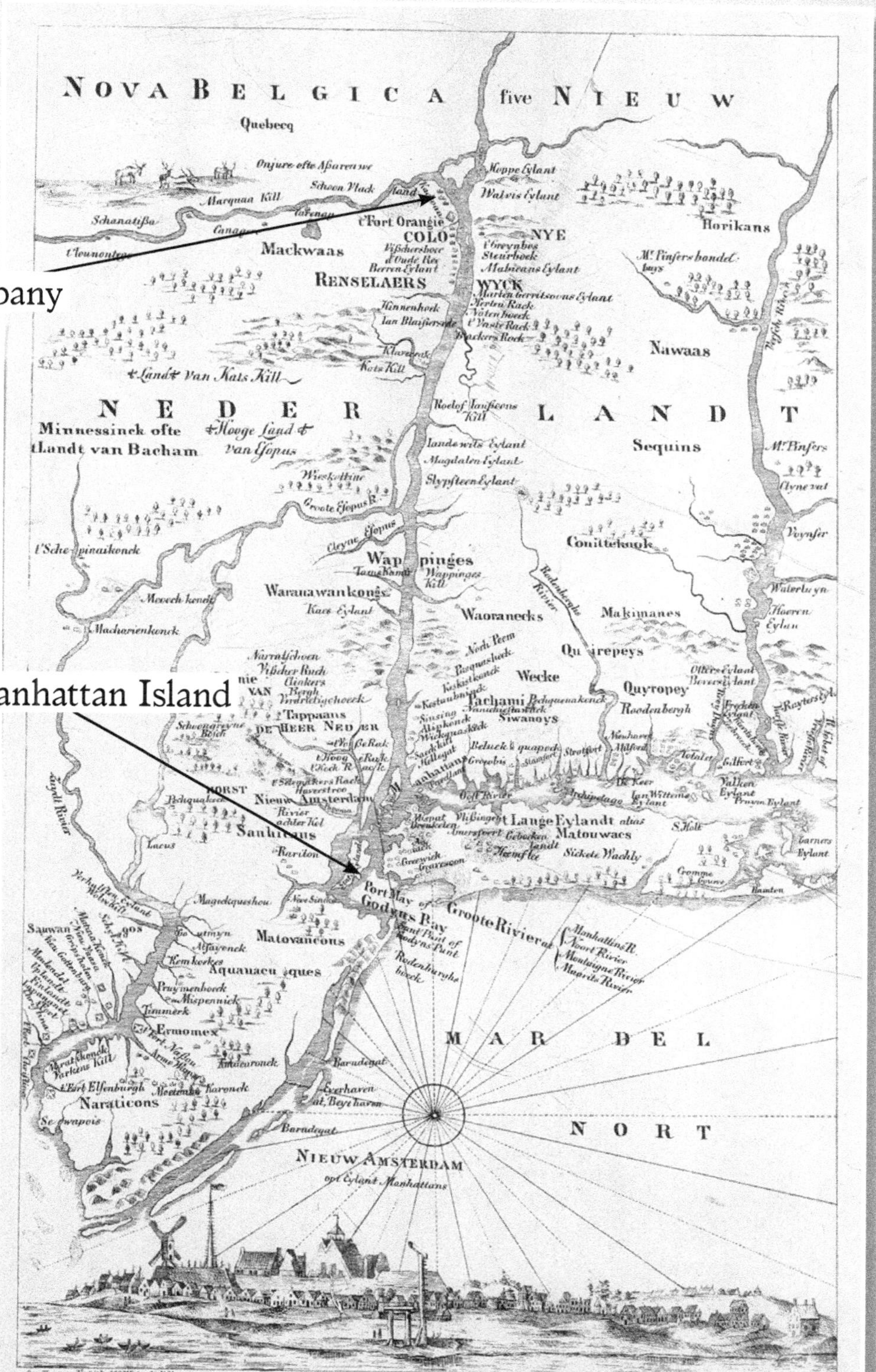

Albany
Manhattan Island
NOVA BELGICA five NIEUW
NEDER LANDT
MAR DEL NORT
NIEUW AMSTERDAM
MAP OF NEW NETHERLAND
With a view of New Amsterdam, (now New-York.) A. D. 1656.

Government During the Revolution

The Declaration of Independence was written and approved in 1776. After that, the colonies became states. The states voted to work together as one nation, but each state also made its own laws and ran its own government.

In 1776, a group of New York's leaders set up the new state government. In early 1777, the first New York constitution was written, approved, and signed.

Next, New Yorkers voted for people to run the state. A man named George Clinton was elected as the first **governor** of New York. Clinton had been a general in George Washington's army and fought against the British. The citizens of New York liked him so much that they reelected him over and over again until 1795.

George Clinton

The large picture shows the first New York State constitution, which was written in 1777. The leaders of New York had to meet in secret to write the constitution. They were afraid they might be captured by the British, who did not want the colonies to form their own government.

51. This Convention therefore in the Name & by the Authority of the Good People of this State doth ordain determin[e] and declare that no Authority shall on any Pretence whatever be exercised over the People or Members of this State but such as shall be derived from and Granted by them. ✗

2 ✗ This Convention doth further in [the Na]me & by the [Authority] of the good [Peo]ple of this State [or]dain determine [and decla]re that the [supreme] Legislative [Power] within this [Sta]te, shall be vested in two sepa-rate & distinct Bodies of men, the one to be called the Assembly of the State of New York the other to be called the Senate of the State of New York [w]ho together shall [for]m the Legisla-[ture] & meet once [a]t least in every [year] for the [dispatch] of [bus]iness

3. And Whereas Laws inconsistant with the Spirit of this Constitution or with the public Good may be has-tily & Unadvisedly passed; Be it Ordained that the Governor for the Time being, the Chancellor & the Judges of the Supreme Court or any two of them, together with the Governor, shall be and hereby are Constituted a Council to revise all Bills about to be passed into Laws by the Legislature. And for that purpose shall assemble themselves from time to time when the Le-gislature shall be Convened; for which Neverthe-less, they shall not receive any Sallary or Conside[ra]-tion under any pretence whatever. And that all Bills which have passed the Senate & Assemb[ly] shall before they become Laws, be presented to the said Council for their revisal & Consideration; an[d] if upon such revision & Consideration it should ap-pear improper to the said Council, or a Majority of them, that the said Bill should become a Law [of] this State, that they return the same together with their Objections there to ~~the same~~ in Writing to the Sena[te or House of] Assembly in which [soever] the same shall have originated [who] shall enter the Objections sent down by the Cou[n]-cil at large in their Minutes & proceed to reconsid[er] the said Bill — But if after such Reconsideration [two] thirds of the said Senate or House of Assembly ~~[illegible]~~ shall Notwithstand[ing] the said Objections agree to pass the same it shall —

Local Government

There are different levels of government. Every state in the United States has its own government. So does every city. They govern different things and have to work together.

The leader of a city government is the **mayor**. Every four years New York City elects a new mayor. New Yorkers also elect a **city council**, much like the council that ran the Iroquois League. The city council runs the city. The mayor makes proposals and appoints officials. The council writes and votes on laws. The mayor and city council work together in City Hall in Manhattan. They are responsible for making sure New York is a good, safe place to live.

Most mayors cannot serve more than two terms. Council members are elected for four years and can only serve twice. Fifty-one council members represent the five different boroughs, or areas, of New York City. The five **boroughs** are Manhattan, Queens, Brooklyn, the Bronx, and Staten Island. Each council member represents about 140,000 people.

New York City's City Hall was built in 1803. In 1858, some fireworks exploded too close to City Hall, and it caught fire. Luckily, only the top part of the building was harmed, and it was quickly rebuilt. This picture from the front page of *Harper's Weekly* shows the crowds that gathered to see the fire. The color photograph shows how City Hall looks today.

HARPER'S WEEKLY
A
JOURNAL OF CIVILIZATION

Vol. II.—No. 87.] NEW YORK, SATURDAY, AUGUST 28, 1858. [Price Five Cents.

THE BURNING OF THE CITY HALL, NEW YORK, AUGUST 18, 1858.

State Government

New York City became the first state capital of New York in 1789. Albany became the state capital in 1797, and it is still New York's capital today. All the representatives of New York State's government meet in Albany.

The state government makes laws for the state. It is also in charge of providing public education, health care, and other important services for its **citizens**, or the people who live in New York State. The money for these comes from taxes that New York citizens pay. The state leaders have to decide how to use the money from taxes. To do this, they make a budget.

The first New York constitution set up the state's government. Like the national government, the state government has three branches, or parts: the **executive** branch, the **legislative** branch, and the **judicial** branch.

The Capitol Building in Albany was finished in 1899. It took 32 years to build! The small picture shows New York State's official seal. Two figures representing Liberty and Justice stand on either side of a scene of sailing ships on a blue river. A bright sun shines over green mountains. A bald eagle, representing the United States, sits on top of a globe. The word "Excelsior" on the banner means "Ever Upward."

THE GREAT SEAL OF THE STATE OF NEW YORK
EXCELSIOR

The Executive Branch

The executive branch plans the state budget and makes sure that all state laws are carried out. The governor of New York is the leader of the executive branch. This person chooses many of the people who help run the state. New York citizens vote for a new governor every four years. There is no limit on the number of times a person can run for governor.

The executive branch includes many **departments**. The **attorney general** goes to court and represents New York in state **trials**. The **treasurer** keeps track of how the state's tax money is spent. Other people are in charge of highway and road safety, public schools, and helping people find jobs.

Since 1875, all the governors of New York and their families have lived in the Executive Mansion in Albany. One of New York's most famous governors was Theodore Roosevelt. He served as governor from 1899 to 1900 and went on to become president of the United States in 1901.

Theodore Roosevelt

The Legislative Branch

The legislative branch makes laws for the state. New York State's legislative branch works the same way as the legislative branch of the national government. Many people have ideas for laws, but only the legislative branch has the power to turn an idea into a law.

New York State's legislative branch has two parts—the **state assembly** and the **state senate**. The assembly has 150 members. The senate has 61 members. The members of the assembly and the senate are elected by the citizens of New York. All members are elected for two-year terms. The assembly and the senate vote to make New York State's laws. Both the senate and the assembly have to pass the law for it to become official.

This picture shows members of the New York State Assembly taking part in a meeting in the Capitol Building in Albany. Albany was chosen to be the capital of New York because of its central location. People from all parts of the state can easily get to Albany.

The Judicial Branch

The judicial branch is New York State's court system. It includes all New York State courts. Within the state, there are different kinds of courts. Each has a judge who is in charge of the courtroom. **Judges** are generally elected by the people. Sometimes they are appointed by the governor. The judge oversees all **cases**. **Juries** decide the outcome of most cases. Being on a jury is an important way for citizens to be a part of New York's government.

State courts only listen to cases that have to do with state laws. They settle disagreements between citizens in the state, decide if someone is guilty of breaking a state law, and decide whether or not state laws follow New York's constitution.

The Court of Appeals is the most powerful court in New York State. People who are unhappy with the decisions made by other New York State courts can ask the Court of Appeals to hear the case again. This picture shows the room where the Court of Appeals meets in the Capitol Building in Albany.

The United States Government

Like New York State, the national government has three branches. The president is the leader of the executive branch. The president makes sure that the country's laws are carried out, leads the military, and meets with leaders of other countries.

The legislative branch is called Congress. Congress makes laws for the whole country. Congress is made up of the Senate and the House of Representatives. Both the Senate and the House have to pass a law for it to become official.

The judicial branch is made up of the national courts. They oversee cases that deal with national laws. The Supreme Court is the most important court in the country. Judges who serve on the Supreme Court are chosen by the president. They decide if the country's laws agree with the U.S. Constitution.

As citizens of our state and our country, we have many rights. The job of our state and national governments is to protect those rights. We also have many responsibilities. We have to make sure our government works well by voting, serving on juries, and letting our leaders know what we think.

Glossary

attorney general: The chief law officer of a nation or state.

boroughs: The five areas that make New York City.

cases: Legal actions that are heard in a court.

citizens: People who live in a city, state, or country.

city council: The legislative body of a city.

clans: Groups of families.

colonies: New lands that are claimed and ruled by another country.

colonists: The people living in a colony.

constitution: A written set of rules by which a state or nation is governed.

Declaration of Independence: A paper approved on July 4, 1776, which states that the American colonies were free from English rule.

democracy: A government that is ruled by its people.

departments: Parts of a government responsible for making policies and making sure they are carried out.

elect: To choose a person for an office or position.

executive: Having to do with the branch of state government led by the governor.

government: A system of ruling a state, country, or community.

governor: A person elected or appointed to manage a region.

independence: Freedom from the control or influence of others.

judges: Persons who oversee court cases.

judicial: Having to do with the branch of government made up of courts.

juries: Groups of selected citizens who make the decision in a court case.

laws: Rules of a state or country.

leaders: People who are in charge of or in command of others.

legend: A story passed down from person to person.

legislative: Having to do with the branch of government that makes laws.

local government: The government of a town or city.

mayor: The chief executive of a city or a town.

merchants: People who buy and sell goods.

nation: A group of people who share a common history, culture, and often, language.

representatives: People chosen to act or speak for other people or communities.

route: A course, way, or path of travel from one place to another.

ruled: Controlled or managed.

state assembly: A part of the legislative branch of the state government.

state senate: A part of the legislative branch of the state government.

treasurer: An officer who oversees state money.

trials: Legal action or processes for deciding rulings, on evidence, in a court.

vote: The act of choosing a leader or law.

Index

Primary Source List

Cover. New York State Capitol Building, Albany. Built 1867–1899 under the direction of four architects. Most of the outside is the work of Henry Hobson Richardson and Leopold Eidlitz.

Page 5. Declaration of Independence. Painting by John Trumbull, around 1786–1819. Now in the Rotunda of the U.S. Capitol.

Page 9. Map of New Netherland. Lithograph by George Hayward, around 1850. Copies of the map and cityscape of New Amsterdam created around 1648 by Adriaen van der Donck, to be included in Remonstrance to be submitted to Dutch government.

Page 11. Draft of New York State constitution. Written in 1777. Now in the New York State Archives, Albany.

Page 11 (inset). Portrait of George Clinton. Engraving by J. C. Buttre, mid-1800s. Based on painting by Ezra Ames, 1814, now in the New-York Historical Society.

Page 13. New York City Hall. Constructed 1803–1812. Designed by John McComb Jr. and Joseph-Francois Mangin. Original copper roof installed in 1811; replaced in 1853; replaced in 1858 due to fire damage.

Page 13 (inset). The Burning of City Hall, New York. Wood engraving, front page of *Harper's Weekly*, August 28, 1858.

Page 17. Executive Mansion, Albany. Built as private home for banker Thomas Olcott in 1856. Purchased by New York State in 1877 for use as governor's home. In 1883, Isaac G. Perry, the last architect to work on the Capitol Building, was hired to renovate the Executive Mansion.

Page 17. (inset). Photograph of Theodore Roosevelt. Taken around 1900, while he was governor of New York.

Page 21. Court of Appeals, New York State Capitol Building, Albany. Designed by Henry Hobson Richardson,1875–1883. Image taken from postcard, ca. 1914, now in the Lake County Museum.

Websites

Due to the changing nature of Internet links, The Rosen Publishing Group, Inc. has developed an online list of websites related to the subjects of this book. This site is updated regularly. Please use this link to access the list: **http://www.rcbmlinks.com/nysh/nybc/gnys**